Alley to Zippy

Cats from A to Z

Mary Elizabeth Salzmann

Consulting Editor, Diane Craig, M.A./Reading Specialist

ABDO
Publishing Company

Published by ABDO Publishing Company, 8000 West 78th Street, Edina, Minnesota 55439. Copyright © 2009 by Abdo Consulting Group, Inc. International copyrights reserved in all countries. No part of this book may be reproduced in any form without written permission from the publisher. Super SandCastle™ is a trademark and logo of ABDO Publishing Company.

Printed in the United States.

Editor: Martha E. H. Rustad
Content Developer: Nancy Tuminelly
Cover and Interior Design and Production: Colleen Dolphin, Mighty Media
Photo Credits: Helmi Flick, Fotosearch, Olga Mogilevets , Biosphoto/Klein J.-L. & Hubert M.-L./Peter Arnold Inc., Shutterstock

Library of Congress Cataloging-in-Publication Data

Salzmann, Mary Elizabeth, 1968-

  Alley to Zippy : cats from A to Z / Mary Elizabeth Salzmann.

    p. cm. -- (Let's learn A to Z)

  ISBN 978-1-60453-493-1

  1. Cats--Juvenile literature. 2. Cat breeds--Juvenile literature. I. Title.

SF445.7.S29 2009

636.8--dc22

                    2008023826

Super SandCastle™ books are created by a team of professional educators, reading specialists, and content developers around five essential components— phonemic awareness, phonics, vocabulary, text comprehension, and fluency— to assist young readers as they develop reading skills and strategies and increase their general knowledge. All books are written, reviewed, and leveled for guided reading, early reading intervention, and Accelerated Reader® programs for use in shared, guided, and independent reading and writing activities to support a balanced approach to literacy instruction.

About Super SandCastle™

Bigger Books for Emerging Readers Grades K–4

Created for library, classroom, and at-home use, Super SandCastle™ books support and engage young readers as they develop and build literacy skills and will increase their general knowledge about the world around them. Super SandCastle™ books are part of SandCastle™, the leading preK–3 imprint for emerging and beginning readers. Super SandCastle™ features a larger trim size for more reading fun.

Let Us Know

Super SandCastle™ would like to hear your stories about reading this book. What was your favorite page? Was there something hard that you needed help with? Share the ups and downs of learning to read. We want to hear from you! Send us an e-mail.

sandcastle@abdopublishing.com

Contact us for a complete list of SandCastle™, Super SandCastle™, and other nonfiction and fiction titles from ABDO Publishing Company.

www.abdopublishing.com • 8000 West 78th Street Edina, MN 55439 • 800-800-1312 • 952-831-1632 fax

This fun and informative series employs illustrated definitions to introduce emerging readers to an alphabet of words in various topic areas. Each page combines words with corresponding images and descriptive sentences to encourage learning and knowledge retention. AlphagalorZ inspires young readers to find out more about the subjects that most interest them!

The "Guess what?" feature expands the reading and learning experience by offering additional information and fascinating facts about specific words or concepts. The "More Words" section provides additional related A to Z vocabulary words that develop and increase reading comprehension.

These books are appropriate for library, classroom, and home use.

Aa

Alley Cat

An alley cat is a cat of unknown breed. An alley cat is usually a stray cat that doesn't belong to anyone.

Guess what?

The Abyssinian breed is believed to have started with a cat named Zula.

Abyssinian

The Abyssinian is one of the oldest cat breeds. Abyssinians look like the cats that were worshipped in ancient Egypt.

Bengal

Bengal cats have spotted fur. Their hind legs are shorter than their front legs.

Chartreux

The Chartreux is a French breed. It is one of the oldest breeds of cat.

Calico

A Calico cat is white with black and tan markings. Many different cat breeds can have calico colors and markings.

Cc

Guess what?

Domestic cats are also called housecats.

Domestic Cat

Domestic cat is a general term used for a cat that is not a member of a recognized breed. There are domestic longhaired cats and domestic shorthaired cats.

7

Dd

Egyptian Mau

The Egyptian Mau has a spotted body and striped tail. Mau means *cat* in Egyptian.

Ee

8

Feline

Feline is the scientific name for the cat family. Lions, tigers, cheetahs, and domestic cats are all felines.

Ff

Gg

Guess what?

All cat breeds with *rex* in the name have curly or wavy fur.

German Rex

German Rex cats have curly fur and whiskers.

Himalayan

Himalayan cats have long fur and blue eyes. The Himalayan breed is a cross between the Siamese and Persian breeds.

11

Ii

Indoor Cat

An indoor cat is a pet cat that is not allowed to go outside. Many people keep their cats indoors so they'll be safe from dogs, cars, and other dangers.

Japanese Bobtail

The Japanese Bobtail has a short, fluffy tail like a rabbit's tail. It is a Japanese good luck symbol.

Jj

Korat

The Korat breed originated in Thailand. The Thai word for Korat is *Si-Sawat*.

Kk

Guess what?

The first LaPerm was named Curly.

LaPerm

LaPerms are a new breed of cat. The first one was born in 1982 in Oregon. They have soft, curly fur.

Ll

Maine Coon

The Maine Coon is the oldest American breed of cat. They are large and have long, shaggy fur.

Mm

16

Guess what?

Norwegian Forest Cats are nicknamed "wegies."

Norwegian Forest Cat

Because they are from a cold climate, Norwegian Forest Cats developed a two-layered coat to keep them warm.

Oo

Ocicat

The Ocicat is a cross between an Abyssinian and a Siamese. It is cream and brown with spots.

Persian

Persians are one of the oldest breeds of cat. They have short legs, large heads, and long fur. Persians can be many different colors.

Pp

Qq

Queen

Adult female cats
are called queens.

20

Ragdoll

Ragdoll cats often relax completely when picked up so they look like floppy dolls. That's how they got the name.

Guess what?

The Ragdoll is the largest domestic breed of cat. Male Ragdolls can weigh more than 20 pounds (9 kg).

Russian Blue

Russian Blue cats have gray-blue fur. Their fur is short and very soft.

Rr

Siamese

Siamese cats are white with dark markings on their ears, face, legs, and tail. They are very vocal and can make a lot of different sounds.

Sphynx

The Sphynx cat is hairless and has very large ears. It originated in Canada.

Ss

22

Tabby

A Tabby cat is either brown, gray, or orange with dark stripes. Many different cat breeds can have Tabby colors and markings.

Turkish Van

Turkish Vans are white with color only on the head and tail. Unlike most cat breeds, Turkish Vans like to swim.

Tt

23

Ural Rex

The Ural Rex breed was discovered in Russia. It was named after the Ural Mountains. Ural Rex kittens are born with gray fur. Their fur changes color as they get older.

Uu

24

Veterinarian

A veterinarian is a doctor who takes care of animals. People take their cats to the veterinarian for checkups and when they get hurt or sick.

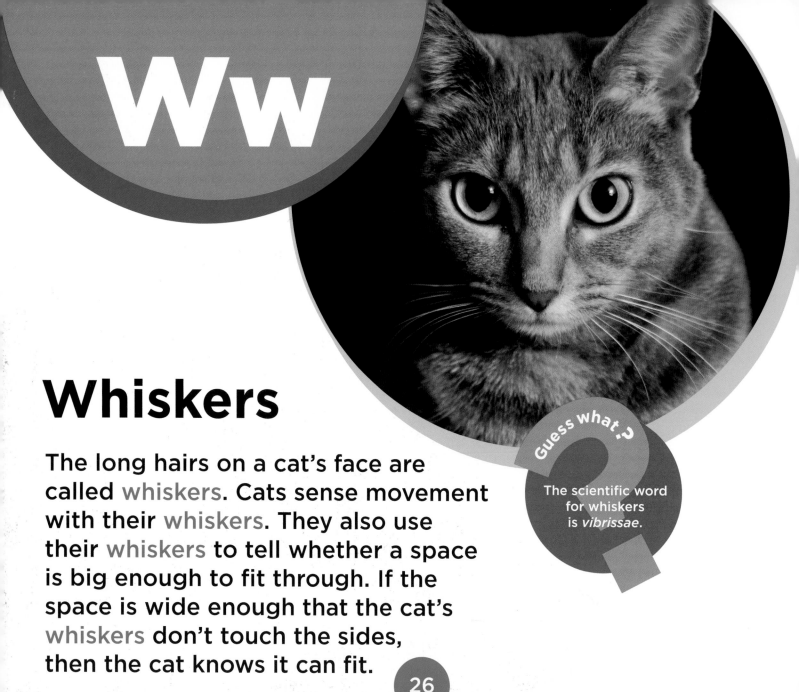

Ww

Whiskers

The long hairs on a cat's face are called whiskers. Cats sense movement with their whiskers. They also use their whiskers to tell whether a space is big enough to fit through. If the space is wide enough that the cat's whiskers don't touch the sides, then the cat knows it can fit.

Guess what?

The scientific word for whiskers is *vibrissae*.

26

ManX

Manx cats do not have tails. They originated on the Isle of Man, between Ireland and England.

27

Yy

Guess what?

York Chocolate cats were first bred in New York state in 1983.

York Chocolate

York Chocolate cats are longhaired cats that are either chocolate brown or lavender, sometimes combined with white. York Chocolates have very fluffy tails.

Zippy Cat

Cats are known for being able to move quickly. They like to zip around chasing toys, string, mice, or bugs.

29

Zz

Glossary

alley – a narrow street or lane between buildings.

ancient – very long ago or very old.

breed – 1) a group of animals or plants that have ancestors and characteristics in common. 2) to raise animals, such as cats, that have certain traits.

checkup – a routine examination by a doctor.

chocolate – a dark brown color.

climate – the usual weather in a place.

develop – to grow or change over time.

domestic – living with or near humans.

female – being of the sex that can produce eggs or give birth. Mothers are female.

hind – located in the back or rear.

lavender – a light grayish-purple or grayish-blue color.

layer – one thickness of a material or a substance lying over or under another.

marking – the usual pattern of color on an animal.

originate – to start or begin.

recognize – to officially accept.

relax – to be at rest or at ease.

stray – having wandered away or gotten lost.

symbol – an object that represents something else.

term – a word or expression used to describe something.

unlike – different or not alike.

usually – commonly or normally.

vocal – talking frequently or loudly.

More Cat Breeds!

Can you learn about these cat breeds too?

American Bobtail	Chinchilla	Red Self
American Curl	Colorpoint Shorthair	Savannah
American Shorthair	Cornish Rex	Scottish Fold
American Wirehair	Devon Rex	Selkirk Rex
Angora	European Shorthair	Siberian
Australian Mist	Exotic Shorthair	Singapura
Birman	Havana Brown	Snowshoe
Bombay	Italian Rex	Sokoke
Brazilian Shorthair	Javanese	Somali
British Shorthair	Munchkin	Tonkinese
Burmese	Nebelung	Tortoiseshell
Burmilla	Oriental Shorthair	Turkish Angora
Chausie	Pewter Longhair	Wild Abyssinian